Self-Publishing FOR THE CLUELESS®

2ND EDITION

the WORKBOOK

EXPANDED! Contains Complete Information on ePublishing

ISBN 978-1-891440-99-1 © 2014 www.RoundsMiller.com

Mike Rounds

Self-Publishing for the Clueless® 2nd Edition
The Workbook

6318 Ridgepath Court
Rancho Palos Verdes, CA 90275-3248
CPMPub@RoundsMiller.com

All rights reserved. No part of this book may be reproduced or transmitted in any form (including, not limited to, in print, online, on a CD, DVD, MP3 or in any other format now known or introduced in the future) with the intention of reselling or distributing such copies without written permission from the publisher, except for brief quotations included in a review.

This book contains excerpted copyrighted material *from Fishin' With A Net 8th Edition, E-Commerce for the Clueless®, Self-Publishing for the Clueless®, E-Publishing for the Clueless®,* and *Trademarks® and Copyrights© for the Clueless®.*

Disclaimer

This book is written with the understanding that the author was not engaged in rendering legal services. The information included has been carefully prepared and is correct to the best of their knowledge as of the publication date. If you require legal or expert advice, the services of professionals should be used. The author disclaims any personal liability, either directly or indirectly, for advice or information presented in this book.

The information as described has been used successfully to obtain savings for some of the people who have used it. Although all efforts have been expended to supply the latest in complete, accurate and up-to-date information, it must be understood that the ultimate success of the user is dependent upon market conditions, efforts expended by the user, and other variable factors that are beyond the control of the authors, and that neither the users' actual expenses nor successes are guaranteed nor implied.

Throughout this book, trademarked names are used. Rather than put a trademark symbol after every occurrence of the trademarked name, we used the names in an editorial fashion only, and to the benefit of the trademark owner, with no intention of infringement of the trademark.

At the time this edition was printed and released, all of the sites listed were active and accessible to anyone having access to the Internet. Neither the author nor the publisher is responsible for broken links, abandoned sites, or changes that are beyond their control.

© 2014 by Mike Rounds
First Printing, 2014
Printed in the United State of America
978-1-891440-99-1

Self-Publishing for the Clueless® 2nd Edition
The Workbook

Table of Contents

Part 1 General Information 1
   What Is Publishing? 1
Part 2 Types of Published Materials 3
Part 3 Publishing Details 7
   The Cover 7
      Sizes of Books 9
      Illustrations, Pictures and Graphics 11
      Headlines and Bullet Points 13
      ISBN 15
      Barcodes 15
      Bookland EAN 15
Part 4 Types of Books, Binding, and Printing Processes 17
   Binding Styles *(aka The Cover)* 17
      Hard Bound 17
      Perfect Binding 17
      3-Ring 17
      Plastic Comb Binding 17
      Plastic Coil Binding 19
      Saddle Stitched 19
   Printing Types 21
      Photocopying (aka the Xerox® machine) 21
      Offset Lithography 21
      Digital Printing 21
      Print-On-Demand (POD) 23
Part 5 E-books 25
   Tablet Computing 25
      What's a Tablet? 25
      E-book Readers 27
      E-Publishing Formats 29
   Amazon's Kindle 29
   Practical E-Publishing 31
   Portable Document Format (PDF) 31
      Multi-Media E-books 33
   How Do You Create An E-Book? 35
Part 6 Distributing and Marketing Your Products 37
   Web Sites, PayPal, and Pay-Per-Download 37
   How To Create A Free E-Commerce Web Site 37
      Creating A Web Site Using Weebly.com 39
      The Things You'll Need On Your Web Site 39
      The Shopping Cart 41
      Pay-Per-Download Service 41
   QR Codes—The Easiest Way To Link People To Your Web Site! 45
   Listing With Major Distribution Chains 47
      Amazon.com 47
Part 7 Legal Stuff 51
   Trademarks 51
   Copyrights 51

Self-Publishing for the Clueless® 2nd Edition
The Workbook

Part 8 Types And Styles Of Books	53
Rapid Ways To Create Information Products	55
Creating A Question And Answer Audio Product	55
How To Publish The World's Least Expensive Printed Book	57
The Acronym Technique for Writing a Book	61
Part 9 Book Categories	65
Part 10 References and Resources	67

About the Author

Mike Rounds of Rounds, Miller and Associates, is a speaker, trainer and author with more than 200 published works. Mike's books are sold by major distributors, including Barnes and Noble, Amazon.com and Baker and Taylor. Mike delivers more than 150 seminars per year, and his students have published more than 2,000 products. He owns a micro-publishing company and is the creator of the "… for the Clueless®" series.

Mike has written and developed dozens of training programs for using the Web and its elements and has delivered over 3,000 seminars and workshops to tens of thousands of participants on the topic of effective Web site design and usage.

He currently offers over 100 programs a year on the topic and his schedule can be viewed at www.RoundsMiller.com.

Mike Rounds
Rounds, Miller and Associates
6318 Ridgepath Court
Rancho Palos Verdes, CA 90275-3248
www.RoundsMiller.com
Mike@RoundsMiller.com
310-544-9502

Self-Publishing for the Clueless® 2nd Edition
The Workbook
Part 1 General Information

What Is Publishing?

Traditionally, publishing is defined as the selection, preparation, and distribution of printed matter—including books, newspapers, magazines, and pamphlets.

A more contemporary definition would be that publishing is making knowledge, information, or experiences available to others though available distribution channels.

What's the difference between royalty publishing and self-publishing?

Royalty publishing: If a company pays for the printing, distribution, and perhaps, some of the promotion, and pays you a percentage of the sales of book (known as a royalty), you are a royalty writer or author.

In traditional publishing, the author completes his or her manuscript, writes a query letter or a proposal, and submits these documents to a publishing house (or has a literary agent do this for them, if an agent can be acquired).

An editor reads the manuscript, considers whether it is right for the house, and decides either to reject it (leaving the author free to offer it to another publisher) or to publish it.

If the publishing house decides to publish the book, the house buys the rights from the writer and pays him or her an advance on future royalties.

The house puts up the money to design and package the book, prints as many copies of the book as it thinks will sell, markets the book, and distributes the finished book to the public.

Self-Publishing: If you pay to have your book produced, you are a self-published author.

An author who decides to self-publish basically becomes the publisher and handles everything including the writing, printing, distribution and promotion of the material.

The author must proofread the final text and provide the funds required to publish the book, as well as the camera-ready artwork.

The author is responsible for marketing and distributing the book, filling orders, and running advertising campaigns.

Self-Publishing for the Clueless® 2nd Edition
The Workbook

Notes:

Self-Publishing for the Clueless® 2nd Edition
The Workbook
Part 2 Types of Published Materials

When we speak about publishing, we usually think about paper books and today, we tend to add e-books to the mix.

But there are actually four types of publishing:

1. Paper or print

2. E-books or electronic print

3. Audio books

4. Video books

The First Decisions

The first thing you must determine is whether your material is going to be privately or publicly distributed.

The second is your choice of the delivery vehicle.

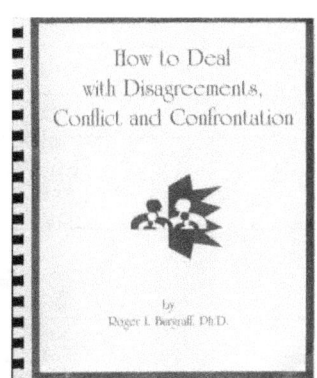

Private distribution, like selling the material from a magazine ad, from your own Web site, creating a workbook for a seminar or workshop doesn't need ISBN bar codes, Library of Congress numbers, formal copyright registration, or a fancy cover.

If the manual is required for the course, like a textbook or workbook, its value is in the content and unless you're just thrilled with creating a fancy item, you don't need to do much past checking it for accuracy and completeness.

On the other hand, if you're going to be publicly offering your material as an optional purchase, regardless of whether it's a private venue, like a back of the room table at a workshop, or putting it on Amazon.com or displaying it in Barnes and Noble, you'll have to put all of the elements together to make an attractive, saleable product including a well-designed cover, formal registration, and all of the appropriate codes and labeling.

Self-Publishing for the Clueless® 2nd Edition
The Workbook

Notes:

Self-Publishing for the Clueless® 2nd Edition
The Workbook

The Four Steps In Publishing

1. Authorship:

- Writing
- Editing
- Cover Design
- Copyright/Trademark filing
- Library of Congress recording
- Boilerplate pages

- Dedication
- Copyright information
- Testimonials
- Index
- Glossary

2. Printing: reproduction of the material for distribution to the buying public

3. Distribution: making the material available to the buying public

4. Promotion: letting the buying public know that the material is available

Self-Publishing for the Clueless® 2nd Edition
The Workbook

Notes:

Self-Publishing for the Clueless® 2nd Edition
The Workbook
Part 3 Publishing Details

The Cover

> *Anyone who believes that a book is NOT judged by its cover has never met a buyer from Barnes and Noble.*
> Pam Shepard
> Barnes and Noble Buyer

On the average, a bookstore browser will spend two to three seconds looking at the front cover and 15 seconds scanning the back cover. E-books are even shorter with an average scanned view of one second or less.

Unless you're specifically dealing with a manual that people are absolutely required to purchase with a class course, seminar, or lecture, a great book cover design is essential because readers, retailers and reviewers glance at a book for only a few seconds before they make a choice.

To be successful, you need to make sure it's your book they're choosing. This includes the book cover itself, a dust jacket (if you've decided to go hardcover), and can include logo design, sell sheets, promo items, business cards, postcards, bookmarks and almost anything else you may need to ensure your book is a success.

Here's the bottom line: Hire a professional to do your cover for you!

Design a Cover or Have One Designed For You!

There are two timeless statements:

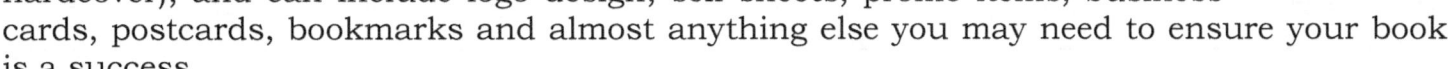

1. You never get a second chance to make a good first impression and

2. A book is judged by its cover.

I'm not generally a great fan of authors producing their own book covers even though I've listed resources below that will help you to do it for very little money.

Book cover design is a specialized form of graphic arts and whether the cover is electronic or paper, it still has to look good and be appealing to the reader, or quite frankly, readers won't bother to purchase or read it.

Here are my recommended resources for creating book covers and 3-D packaging:

Self-Publishing for the Clueless® 2nd Edition
The Workbook

Notes:

Self-Publishing for the Clueless® 2nd Edition
The Workbook

A desktop publishing program such as Microsoft Publisher will allow you to try different designs and concepts and make your own book cover. A variety of their book layout templates are at http://tinyurl.com/ktpvxzd.

Purchase a do it yourself professional book cover authoring software from Book Cover pro for $187 www.bookcoverpro.com/index.html.

Now, having said all that, my recommendation is to you use a professional cover designer like Leslie Sears at www.LesIsMore.us; Leslie@LesisMore.us; 310-245-6411. You'll get spectacular results for a minimal investment and no problems.

The Title and Category

If possible, try to title your book so that it reflects the content or topic in some manner or another.

The Category Title

Because books are catalogued, shelved, and electronically listed by their category, you must add the category title to your book cover so that you get shelved in the appropriate place.

The category title is usually placed in the upper left-hand corner on the back cover of a printed book and is used as the category reference when listing an e-book in an online catalog.

There's a complete list of the categories currently being used in the publishing industry in the back of this workbook. It has grown from a starting list of 34 categories in 2005 to hundreds of categories as of this date of printing.

Sizes of Books

The display characteristics, end usage for the book, and practical economics should be your guideline here.

If you envision your book on the retail shelves, a smaller size tends to be better because it doesn't take up a lot of shelf space.

5½" x 8½", 6" x 8" or 7" x 9" are currently very popular and could be considered a standard. On the other hand, training manuals and how to books, regardless of where they are offered, lend themselves to the larger size of 8½" x 11" in order to get everything included as clearly as possible without cramping the material or making the font sizes too small to be read easily.

Self-Publishing for the Clueless® 2nd Edition
The Workbook

Notes:

Self-Publishing for the Clueless® 2nd Edition
The Workbook

Special note: If you're doing an e-book, such as a manual, and you're supplying it is either a CD file or a downloadable file and you suspect that people are going to print it out as well as read on screen, the most effective size will be 8½" x 11" because this is the standard paper that people have in their printer.

Illustrations, Pictures and Graphics

This part of printing and publishing is undergoing a radical change because of the new electronic formats and printing methods.

Color Photos

What we commonly associate with black and white imagery is actually what's known as halftone grey or combination of black, white, and eight shades of gray.

This became common in our everyday life because of black and white television which actually does reproduce these 10 shades ranging from black to white.

Most commercial printing processes have no problem producing these 10 shades of gray on just about any kind of paper that you choose to use.

When you decide to convert your book to an e-book, most publishing formats have

Color **Half-Tone Grey Scale** **Black and White**

no problem if handling halftone grey, black and white, and even full color because the displays on computers are designed to accommodate full color and high-resolution graphics.

The one exception to this is any e-book reader that uses a technology called E ink. These include the Kindle, the Nook, the KOBO Glo, and the Sony e-reader.

Because E Ink technology is extremely low-power, the readers that use the technology usually have a battery life of a month or longer.

The trade-off is that the E Ink technology, which consists of a matrix of little electronic marbles that are black on one side and white on the other, restricts the graphics display characteristics to strictly black-and-white which causes halftone gray images to look strange and full color images to become unrecognizable.

Self-Publishing for the Clueless® 2nd Edition
The Workbook

Notes:

Self-Publishing for the Clueless® 2nd Edition
The Workbook

If you are planning on having your book formatted and distributed for one of these readers, pay close attention to the graphics content and if there's any way possible for you to compensate for their display inequities or to leave the graphics out in these formats, by all means do so because the blurry or distorted images will severely detract from your publication.

Headlines and Bullet Points

According to the world's leading experts, 80 percent of the people who read ONLY read headlines and bullet points and skip over the details and written copy!

Think about a newspaper—if the headline does NOT get your attention, you will NOT bother to look at or read the article.

The supermarket tabloids are an even better example where the headline is in 72 point type and is written so that you are compelled to read it:

I Watched An Alien Hypnotize My Pet Chicken!

In a book about the history of the tabloids, both Randolph Hurst and Rupert Murdoch admitted that the headlines were the key to selling newspapers and the copy could be filled in later.

Both the tile and the chapter headers of your book must attract the attention of the reader or only the most dedicated of readers will read the material.

Your headlines MUST:

- Attract attention (using interesting, active words).
- Connect to ordinary readers (be easily understood).

If you have trouble writing headlines and bullet points, we recommend the **Headline Creator Pro Suite.** This simple program asks you to answer four questions about the topic and then automatically creates hundreds of headlines that you can use or modify in any written work.

It's available at www.rmacart.com/business-support-software.html.

Self-Publishing for the Clueless® 2nd Edition
The Workbook

Notes:

Self-Publishing for the Clueless® 2nd Edition
The Workbook

ISBN

If you are a new publisher and need one or more ISBNs, the agency responsible for assigning these numbers in the US is www.Bowker.com.

The ISBN (International Standard Book Number) is a unique 10-digit number that identifies one title or edition of a title from one specific publisher and is unique to that edition. As the official ISBN Agency for the United States, Bowker (www.bowker.com) is responsible for the assignment of the ISBN Publisher Prefix to those publishers with a residence or office in the US who are publishing their titles within the US.

Barcodes

Bar codes are those vertical lines on the back of books and have become a requirement by most of the book trade. This enables a price scanner to identify the title, ISBN number and price. There are many barcodes but the one used to mark books is called the *Bookland* bar code and follows a specific format used exclusively with books.

Bookland EAN

There are several different bar code systems in the United States. In order to sell your book in a bookstore, the standard is the EAN Bookland bar code (for ISBN numbers).

Bowker offers a bar code service and once a bar code is made, it cannot be revised. If you want to change the price of an item, you must purchase a new bar code.

Bowker will create one for you for an additional $25 and most professional cover designers have the software to do it for about the same price.

For ANY commercial distribution of your book, you will be required to have an ISBN so the organization can catalog it in their computer system. For a printed book, you will need the bar code so that it can be physically scanned for inventory and sales purposes.

Self-Publishing for the Clueless® 2nd Edition
The Workbook

Notes:

Self-Publishing for the Clueless® 2nd Edition
The Workbook
Part 4 Types of Books, Binding, and Printing Processes

Binding Styles (aka The Cover)

Hard Bound

Hardbound books have a hard back, cover, and spine and most are case bound. This provides a stiff cover and binding edge, as well as allowing the binding edge to open easily.

Because of the costs involved, most self-published books are not hard bound.

Perfect Binding

Perfect Binding

Paperback books are an example of perfect binding. The cover is a stiff paper that is wrapped around the pages forming a spine, front, and back covers.

They're held together by a flexible adhesive which keeps its strength and resiliency for a long period of time. This binding is great for many types of books, including manuals, workbooks, novels and collections of short stories.

3-Ring

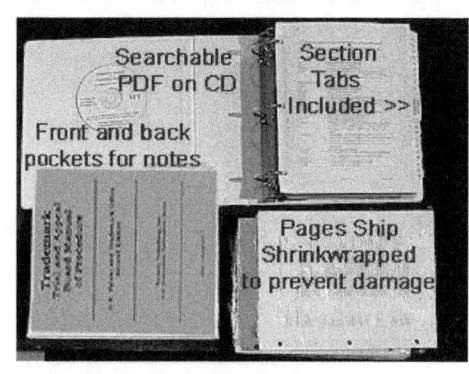

3-Ring binding is a good option for books that must lay open flat or where you're adding a lot of custom or updated materials on an irregular basis.

3-Ring binding is something that you can do for short runs of books or for custom designed books such as manuals and workbooks.

Plastic Comb Binding

Plastic comb binding (also known as GBC binding) is used for books which must lie flat, such as manuals, how-to books, or workbooks.

Self-Publishing for the Clueless® 2nd Edition
The Workbook

Notes:

Self-Publishing for the Clueless® 2nd Edition
The Workbook

You can choose from different comb colors to coordinate with your cover.

Although you can have your books comb bound produced rapidly at your local office supply store, it's expensive because its labor intensive since all of the punching and comb assembly is done by hand.

Plastic Coil Binding

Plastic coil binding is another style that is ideal for books that must lay open flat. The main advantage of plastic coil binding is that the book can be folded in half.

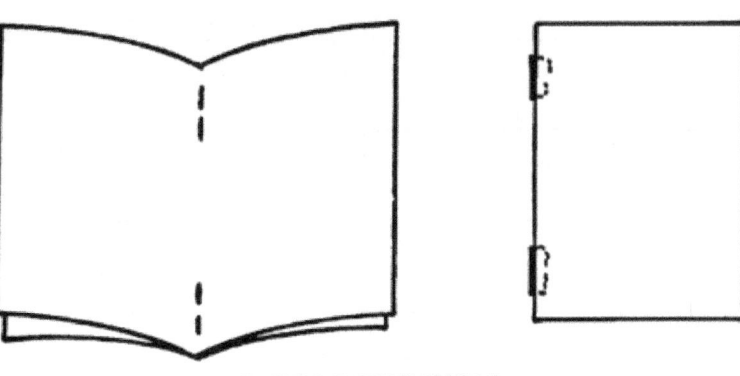

This binding is similar to wire binding except it's made of more durable plastic. These are usually available in a black or white plastic coil to coordinate with your cover.

Like comb binding, you can have your coil bound books produced rapidly at your local office supply store, but it's expensive because its labor intensive since all of the punching and comb assembly is done by hand.

Although your local stationary supply store is expensive when it comes to coil binding, there are now commercial printer/binder facilities (like the ones in our reference section) who will coil bind smaller quantities starting at 100-150 books at a reasonable price.

Saddle Stitched

Saddle stitched is a method of securing loose printed pages with staples down the middle of a folded sheaf of papers. Many booklets are saddled stitched.

Note: Side-stitching is a similar method where the pages are stapled about 1/4" from the spine.

SADDLE STITCHING

Comic books and mail order catalogs with 20-30 sheets of paper are an excellent example of saddle stitching with staples that works.

Self-Publishing for the Clueless® 2nd Edition
The Workbook

Notes:

Self-Publishing for the Clueless® 2nd Edition
The Workbook

Printing Types

Photocopying (aka the Xerox® machine)

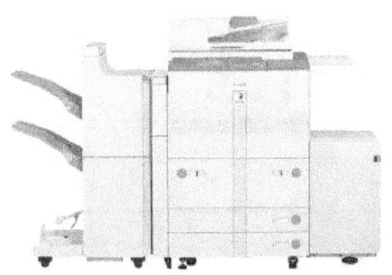

We've grown up with the photocopying machines all around us and as a result we tend to think of them when someone uses the word *printing*.

They're fast, high quality, easy to use, and convenient since you can find them at your local stationary supply store.

The truth is that for short runs of something that you need in a hurry you can't beat the technology. The problem is that speed costs and for any kind of commercial application, you probably can't afford the convenience that this technology offers.

Offset Lithography

The most common printing method in the printing industry, most printers use offset lithography to save on ink and limit set up time.

What this print process does is to create a negative print plate of the material to be reproduced to offset the ink (thus, the name) from these metal printing plates to a rubber cylinder and then transfer it onto the paper stock.

Once the initial set up has been completed, the press cranks out copies at a blinding speed and at print quantities of 5,000 or more books; you can't get a better or cheaper solution.

Hence, you are able to avail of a more affordable and cost effective print job for your color printing requirements.

Digital Printing

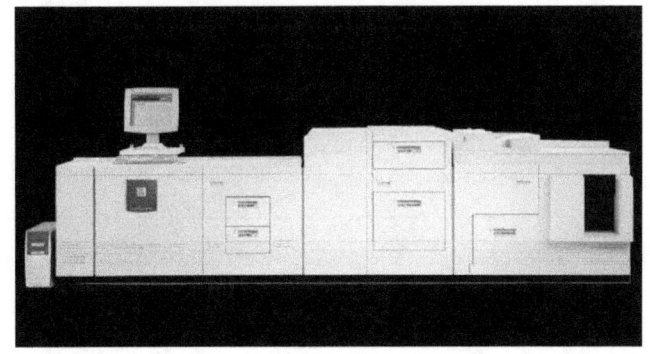

This has probably become the most popular printing method since its introduction and the least understood—primarily because it's been confused with Print-On-Demand or POD!

Digital printing is very effective since it reduces the time to complete the printing process. Think of it as a high speed Xerox machine and collation system on steroids.

Self-Publishing for the Clueless® 2nd Edition
The Workbook

Notes:

Self-Publishing for the Clueless® 2nd Edition
The Workbook

It doesn't need films, plates, or set up because what it does is to transfer the digital file directly to the printing press with the help of a computer.

For short-run, fast-turnaround jobs it's the best system available. Its limitations include color, paper choices, and quality. But not for long—the technology is exploding!

Print-On-Demand (POD)

Print-On-Demand (POD) is a printing technology and business process in which new copies of a book (or other document) are not printed until an order has been received, which means books can be printed one at a time.

Print-On-Demand with digital technology is used as a way of printing items for a fixed cost per copy, regardless of the size of the order.

While the unit price of each physical copy printed is higher than with offset printing, the average cost is lower for very small print runs, because set up costs are much higher for offset printing.

POD has other business benefits besides lower costs (for small runs):

- Technical set-up is usually quicker than for offset printing.

- Large inventories of a book or print material do not need to be kept in stock, reducing storage, handling costs, and inventory accounting costs.

- There is little or no waste from unsold products.

These advantages reduce the risks associated with publishing books and prints and can lead to increased choice for consumers.

However, the reduced risks for the publisher can also mean that quality control is less rigorous than usual especially if the POD process uses a high speed Inkjet printing process instead of a dry toner process.

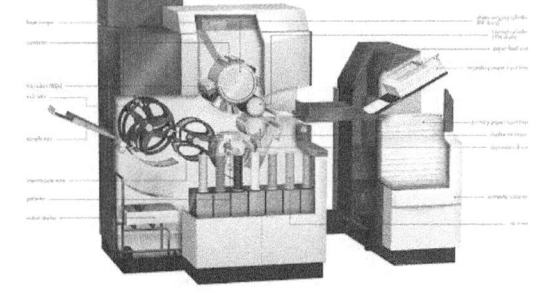

POD printers that use an Inkjet printer are saddled with the ink being wet when the finished book is inserted into a sealed envelope, which tends to smudge and the entire book warps producing a poor quality look to the finished product so make sure you're getting a dry toner process.

Self-Publishing for the Clueless® 2nd Edition
The Workbook

Notes:

Self-Publishing for the Clueless® 2nd Edition
The Workbook
Part 5 E-books

What is e-Publishing? Wikipedia defines electronic publishing or e-Publishing as the digital publication of e-books and electronic articles, and the development of digital libraries and catalogues.

More simply stated e-Publishing is making your creative work available in a format other than ink on paper.

E-books are a growing craze because people are living more portable lives and need devices to keep up with their fast paced lives including tablet computers, cell phones, iPods, MP3 players, digital cameras, and even books.

Where e-Publishing takes a radical departure is in the printing and distribution sections because instead of printing a lot of paper books and delivering them to brick and mortar bookstores, we copy and store the published materials on a Web site and deliver them electronically through the World Wide Web.

These two elements have historically represented a huge expense for the publisher which, in many cases, has prohibited them from getting their work to the public.

Publishing Vs E-Publishing

Element	Physical	EBook
Writing	The Author	
Duplication	Printed Paper	Electronic
Distribution	Brick & Mortar	Web
Promotion	The Author	

Now, with the minimal expense involved in electronic reproduction and distribution, these same authors are enjoying global distribution of their work without having to bankrupt themselves to do so.

Tablet Computing

What's a Tablet?

A tablet is either a pad computer which has a screen size anywhere from 4" to 7" or a tablet computer which as a screen size that's approximately 10" to 12".

They generally have no keyboard and use a touch screen to activate commands, including an on-screen keyboard that allows the user to type letters and numbers.

Although there have been a variety of pad and tablet computers over the years, with varying degrees of acceptance, Apple's iPad created a new sensation and now the product is somewhat universally accepted by the public.

Self-Publishing for the Clueless® 2nd Edition
The Workbook

Notes:

Self-Publishing for the Clueless® 2nd Edition
The Workbook

Although tablet computers lack the power and versatility of a laptop computer, they're actually a brilliant idea due on the fact that there are a lot more people who read information than those who write information.

How many different ones are there?

As of January 2016, there over 5,000 different varieties of tablet computers including e-book readers, simple tablet computers, and tablet computers running Windows 8.

The current predictions say that within 12 months there will be over 6,500 variations and that the price point will drop to approximately 50 percent of what it is today.

E-book Readers

Kindle isn't the only game in town for reading e-books. There are currently over four thousand different tablets and e-book readers available.

- Over 500 new versions are being added each year

- They range in size from 7" to 11" in display size and in cost from $35 to $1,500

- Predictions show that a 7" tablet will soon be available at $30 or less

- E-books can be read on a Windows PC or a Macintosh computer

- E-books can be read on cell phones with large displays

- Some readers, like the Amazon Kindle, can only read their proprietary format

- Some readers, like a computer, iPad, or more sophisticated tablet computer, can read most formats once they have installed the specific software for the format.

- Approximately 60 percent of the adult population of the United States has a smart phone, a tablet computer, or both

- 76 percent of the US population has a computer

The bottom line: Tablets and E-books are here to stay!

You can find a current directory of e-book readers at http://tinyurl.com/dxvdnbf.

You can find a current directory of tablet computers at http://tinyurl.com/jwp37g2.

Self-Publishing for the Clueless® 2nd Edition
The Workbook

Notes:

Self-Publishing for the Clueless® 2nd Edition
The Workbook

E-Publishing Formats

Not all e-books are created equal!

Because of advertising and notoriety, the buying public has become *brand washed*.

From a practical standpoint, being *brand washed* means that we equate everything in a product category with a specific brand of that product.

The three big BRAND formats:
1. **E-Book Reader – Kindle** *(Amazon.com)*
2. **TABLET - I-Pad** *(Apple)*
3. **PDF** *(The rest of the world of E-books and tablet computing!)*

In the world of e-Publishing, this has primarily resulted in e-book readers being called a Kindle (Amazon.com's brand) and a tablet computer being referred to as an iPad, (which is Apple computer's brand).

More importantly, this brand washing has created the mistaken notion that the best and perhaps only way to be e-published is to be listed on Amazon's Kindle.

You may not be aware of it, but there are thousands of different ways to read an e-book and a variety of different formats for offering your materials.

Amazon's Kindle

The Kindle system is a cleverly designed, easy to use system—at least for the user.

For authors and publishers it's a very strict and structured format.

In order to make the Kindle products readable on a variety of devices, Amazon created free Kindle reader software for a variety of platforms.

When a Kindle purchase is made and the e-book is downloaded, the resident software assembles the Kindle parts and pieces into an e-book that is perfectly formatted for the specific device.

In order for this system to work with all of the different e-book reader formats, the author's book must be *disassembled* and formatted to Kindle's strict guidelines so that the pieces that are downloaded have no pre-configuration or bias that would interfere with the specific device's software programs.

Self-Publishing for the Clueless® 2nd Edition
The Workbook

Notes:

Self-Publishing for the Clueless® 2nd Edition
The Workbook

Because of rapid changes in technology, we recommend that you look up the latest information about formatting your e-book for Kindle can be found at their Web site at: https://kdp.amazon.com/self-publishing/help?topicId=A17W8UM0MMSQX6.

Practical E-Publishing

The fastest, easiest, cheapest and most widely used system in the world for creating and distributing electronic documents is PDF.

Portable Document Format (PDF)

Portable Document Format (PDF) is a document exchange created by Adobe Systems in 1993. PDF provides files in a two-dimensional layout that work independent of some software and operating systems.

You must have a specialized (FREE) PDF reader on your computer to view a PDF file.

Pros of PDFs

PDF is currently the most widely used electronic document format worldwide.

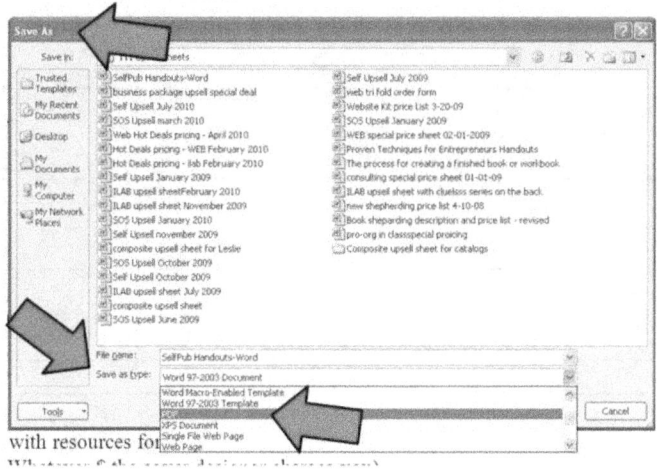

There are a lot of advantages to working in PDF format. PDF files give you control over layout and fonts. They can be generated by GUI-based tools from a number of companies beyond Adobe.

For example, Microsoft Word has the ability to produce PDF files.

The Adobe PDF reader software is free and comes installed on most computers.

Convert the Cover and Body Text to PDF

For all of the hype and rhetoric about Kindle, EPUB and all the great new technological breakthroughs that are becoming available in the world of e-Publishing, no matter what method of final distribution format you use, you'll probably need to convert your book to PDF.

Self-Publishing for the Clueless® 2nd Edition
The Workbook

Notes:

Self-Publishing for the Clueless® 2nd Edition
The Workbook

PDF is a form of snapshot software that is universally readable by both the Windows and Macintosh system and virtually every computer and tablet sold comes with a free PDF reader from Adobe.

If it doesn't, all you do is go to www.adobe.com and download and install the free reader for your computer system.

PDF is the one of the best formats for books where layout is critical to the readability and enjoyment of the book.

PDF is universally supported on most PCs and many e-book reading devices. While the reading experience may suffer from the aforementioned limitations, at least you know it'll work.

PDF is a familiar format. Some percentage of readers still believe that "PDF = E-book," end of story.

Be sure to put a statement and link on any PDF document telling people where they can download and install the free reader software if they don't have it.

Multi-Media E-books

Adding video, sound, and interactive content transforms PDFs into multidimensional communication tools that increase interest and engagement in your documents.

All multimedia that is developed in Flash as well as multimedia that is H.264 compliant can be played back in Adobe Reader 9 and later. (H.264, also known as MPEG-4, is a video compression standard that provides high quality video without substantially increasing file size.) Video files of varying formats and filename extensions can be H.264 compliant.

NOTE: Be sure and check out the section on Multi-media publishing in the complete manual on the CD. Adobe Acrobat Version X Allows you to create a PDF e-book that contains text, graphics, audio, and video which none of the other media allows!

Although Adobe acrobat is the standard, (www.adobe.com) here are some other PDF compilers:

Nuance PDF http://www.nuance.com/for-business/by-solution/pdf/index.htm

Primo PDF www.primopdf.com/index.aspx

PDF995 www.pdf995.com

Self-Publishing for the Clueless® 2nd Edition
The Workbook

Notes:

Self-Publishing for the Clueless® 2nd Edition
The Workbook

CutePDF www.cutepdf.com

DocuDesk www.docudesk.com

PDFill www.pdfill.com

PDF Convertor contained in the Microsoft Office suite

How Do You Create An E-Book?

There are a variety of ways to create e-books and e-Publish for free or very little money.

To create a text style e-book, you write your book using a computer and a word processor.

Here's a short overview of the e-book process:

1. Write your book using *Word,* or whatever word processor you prefer.

2. Insert charts, graphs, photos, clip art (royalty free), and graphics you need to complete the book.

3. Design a cover or have one designed for you.

4. Convert the cover and body text to PDF.

5. Convert the book to the format mandated by the distribution device (such as EPUB for the iPad).

6. Distribute your e-book.

Self-Publishing for the Clueless® 2nd Edition
The Workbook

Notes:

Self-Publishing for the Clueless® 2nd Edition
The Workbook
Part 6 Distributing and Marketing Your Products

Web Sites, PayPal, and Pay-Per-Download

If there's a hot topic these days, it's got to be e-commerce or selling stuff from your Web site.

There is a formal definition of e-commerce that reads something like this: *E-commerce is replacing face to face business relationships with the tools of technology.*

For all practical purposes, most people would say that *e-commerce is buying something from a Web site using a credit card for payment.*

To get involved in e-commerce, you must have the following items:

1. A Web site, preferably one of your own

2. The ability to accept and process all forms of credit cards

3. A shopping cart for visitors, to place their orders with a credit card

4. The option of a pay-per-download capability to sell/deliver e-books and other digitally stored materials

How To Create A Free E-Commerce Web Site

Let's get real, in today's digitally connected world you MUST have a Web site as a place to promote your book and, if you're really serious, to sell both the printed book and a downloadable e-book!

Although there have been ways to create a free Web site since the Web began, few of the methods were free, easy, or comprehensive enough to do most people any good.

What's more, it shouldn't be so complicated that you have to take a course in HTML programming in order to use it which, incidentally, is what many of the *free* offers require.

After listening to a lot of feedback from our seminar attendees and reading a lot of reviews about how expensive and complex it was to create a simple Web site, we found that there

Self-Publishing for the Clueless® 2nd Edition
The Workbook

Notes:

Self-Publishing for the Clueless® 2nd Edition
The Workbook

are several places to create free Web sites that are not a scam in terms of their functionality as well as their ease of usage.

Of course, if the Web site doesn't do what you need it to do; it's not worth anything either so we set out with the following basic criteria understanding that the more exotic features could be added for a price, so based on our research, we recommend www.weebly.com.

The Weebly Web site builder is simple, uncluttered and easy to use, and that's exactly what people with limited technical skills need when it comes to creating your own Internet presence.

Added to this, Weebly's price/performance ratio is one of the best on the market: you can build up to 10 completely separate Web sites on the Pro plan.

Creating A Web Site Using Weebly.com

Weebly.com is a Web site where anyone with basic word processing skills can create a Web site at no cost.

No special software is required and there are no hosting fees for the basic site and less than $7 bucks a month for your own domain name and all of the professional features you ever want or need.

The Things You'll Need On Your Web Site

An author's Web site is NOT a 500 page brochure. It's basically the same kind of information that we've traditionally put into an advertising sheet and order form.

The difference is that now it's electronic and easy to get to and use.

The basic elements include a page or two each with the following topics:

- About the author
- About the book
- Order the book
- Contact the author/publisher
- Feedback form or BLOG

Self-Publishing for the Clueless® 2nd Edition
The Workbook

Notes:

Self-Publishing for the Clueless® 2nd Edition
The Workbook

The Shopping Cart

If you're kind of technically savvy and like modifying your own Web site, you can create a shopping cart, order form, and credit card link system all by yourself.

If, on the other hand, you're more interested in writing and making money than tinkering with technology, you'll be happy to know that everything has been done for you so all you have to do is follow the directions to be successful.

Services like PayPal (www.paypal.com) provide everything you'll need to install a comprehensive shopping cart on your Web site including the ability to process the client's credit card order complete with tax, shipping, and a variety of other calculations if needed.

The big advantage of PayPal is that you're simply *brokering* the business and they actually handle the transaction for you.

This means you don't have to undergo financial vetting and since it's technically their processing efforts, it's free and they don't charge any fees or percentages except when a transaction is actually made.

At this point, you can plan on them keeping about three percent of the total transaction for their services.

Pay-Per-Download Service

For as long as the Web has been around, there has been a process called pay-per-download that allows the visitor to enter their credit card and download software, audio, video, and any form of electronically deliverable material

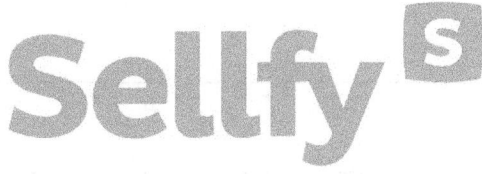

A new service has been integrated into PayPal that provides this once very expensive service to virtually anybody who wants to use it. It's called E-Junkie and it's available from www.Sellfy.com.

The philosophy is quite simple: (Note: You'll still need your PayPal account to handle the money☺)

1. You register with Sellfy

2. You fill out their application (It's FREE!)

3. You upload the material to be sold via download

Self-Publishing for the Clueless® 2nd Edition
The Workbook

Notes:

Self-Publishing for the Clueless® 2nd Edition
The Workbook

4. Sellfy provides a link to the pay-per-download site so that you can put it on your Web page. When the visitor wants to buy a downloadable item, such as audio, video, software, or a database, they simply click on the button and they will be linked to the E-Junkie site.

- When a purchase is made using their system, PayPal charges the purchaser and subtracts a percentage of the purchase price as a handling fee.

- They then direct the purchaser to a coded Web site address to download your e-book to their computer so that they can read it or print it at their discretion.

- PayPal notifies you via e-mail that a transaction has occurred and the funds are available for you to transfer to your bank account.

This is the same kind of system that iTunes and other related MP3 music systems.

The system has several different plans based solely on the amount of storage space you're going to use or the number of products you're going to offer. Their fees are FREE but they take 5% of the total sale..

The best part is that it's free whether you sell one or a million downloads each month so starting out with a free PayPal account and a free Sellfy account will put you in the pay-per-download business for free.

Once you're done, you'll have e-Published your e-book and made it available for sale.

The truly great part about the e-Publishing process is that once you've done the original work, you can keep selling the electronic files over and over again with no printing or postage costs!

There are a great many other ways to advertise and promote your books and e-books.

Book Marketing for the Clueless shows you dozens of different ways that you can do yourself or pay others to do for you.

It's available at www.rmacart.com/audiobooks-with-pdf-manuals.html

Self-Publishing for the Clueless® 2nd Edition
The Workbook

Notes:

Self-Publishing for the Clueless® 2nd Edition
The Workbook
QR Codes—The Easiest Way To Link People To Your Web Site!

Before you print cards or any more promotional material, you MUST look into putting QR codes on them.

These are the little checkerboard squares that are popping up on everything from postcards to magazine ads to business cards to posters.

They are coded checkerboards that can be read by a smart phone or a tablet computer using a free app.

Once scanned, the smart phone or tablet will automatically do what has been programmed into them.

You can make a QR code for FREE that links back to you Web site. The overview about what they are is at http://tinyurl.com/3nbbylc.

To create your own for FREE, go to www.QRStuff.com and use their free online code generator. It's a JPEG graphic so all you have to do is copy and paste them onto anything and everything.

QR Code Readers

To find a FREE QR Code Readers App, go to your device's AP Store and type in: FREE QR Reader app for XXX where XXX is the name of your device. You'll find a number of them so pick the one that seems to work best for you.

Here are two examples of QR codes for our materials. The first one is for our corporate Web site and the second one is for one of the author's YouTube demo videos.

The operative statement here is: "new tools, old rules."

Self-Publishing for the Clueless® 2nd Edition
The Workbook

Notes:

Self-Publishing for the Clueless® 2nd Edition
The Workbook

The summation of this approach is simply stated by saying that we are better off advertising our Web sites in places where we are reasonably sure that our prospective clients are going to be able to see the advertisement and respond to it rather than dropping it into a massive bucket of millions of URLs and hoping that the prospective client fishes ours out.

Listing With Major Distribution Chains

In order to be listed by any online retailers you must have an ISBN number for your book (www.Bowker.com) and a bar code (bar codes are also available from Bowker or professional book cover designers).

Amazon.com

The first word anyone says when we talk about books and distribution is Amazon.com so let's see what they have to offer us.

Amazon Advantage is a self-service consignment program that enables you to promote and sell media products directly on Amazon.com.

Advantage is designed specifically for publishers, music labels, studios, authors, and other content owners who would like to source their products to Amazon.com, the world's leading online retailer.

It gives you the opportunity to market your products to millions of customers. The program offers a proven means of distribution and order fulfillment for media product (such as books, videos, and music).

The Advantage program is not intended for individuals selling used copies, or resellers of books (such as bookstores). If that's your interest, you should review the other selling options, such as Selling on Amazon and Fulfillment by Amazon.

To join Advantage you'll need to set up an Advantage account online.

- Go to http://tinyurl.com/yalnram for all the details.

- Once your account is active, you can start adding the items you intend to source to Amazon Advantage.

- Adding items to your account tells Advantage which products are available from you.

- To list products, you need to have valid legal title to distribute them.

Self-Publishing for the Clueless® 2nd Edition
The Workbook

Notes:

Self-Publishing for the Clueless® 2nd Edition
The Workbook

- Once your titles are enrolled (listed) in your account, Amazon.com will automatically begin ordering them.

- This typically occurs once a week.

- Their goal is to have you send them enough copies of the title to meet current customer demand, along with enough extra to meet that demand for the next few weeks.

- You simply confirm the orders in your Advantage account, and let us know when you anticipate them arriving at our warehouse.

- Information on shipping rules and guidelines can be found in the online Help Center of your Advantage account.Amazon.com.

Check out the full details on the CD Book for information and details about listing with many other locations in both the print and electronic categories.

Self-Publishing for the Clueless® 2nd Edition
The Workbook

Notes:

Self-Publishing for the Clueless® 2nd Edition
The Workbook
Part 7 Legal Stuff

Trademarks

A trademark is the mark of your trade or how your goods and services come to be known and recognized. From a practical standpoint they are a word, symbol, slogan, or even a distinctive sound, which identifies and distinguishes the goods and services of one party from those of another.

The clutter dude and name *Clutterology®* shown at the right is an example of a registered trademark. They belong to Nancy Miller, the owner and creator of the book and training program *Clutterology® Getting Rid of Clutter and Getting Organized* and she, and she alone, can use these marks or authorize others to use them. Incidentally, the registered mark includes the graphic character clutter dude, the name (Clutterology®) or both when they are used together.

Clutterology®

Copyrights

Copyright gives the creator of original works of authorship the exclusive rights to make copies or to authorize others to make copies. Copyrights are technically defined as original works of authorship and are automatically granted upon the fixing (creation) of an idea in fixed or tangible form.

They currently last for the life of the author plus 80 years.

They Cover or protect:

- Literary works
- Musical works, including any accompanying words.
- Dramatic works, including any accompanying music.
- Pantomimes and choreographic works.
- Pictorial, graphic, and sculptural works.
- Motion pictures and other audiovisual works.
- Sound and video recordings include live, unedited tape or camcorder recordings.
- Architectural works which are defined as such works as blueprints.

Self-Publishing for the Clueless® 2nd Edition
The Workbook

Notes:

Self-Publishing for the Clueless® 2nd Edition
The Workbook
Part 8 Types and Styles of Books

Writing styles vary and should be based on the people who you are writing for (AKA the readers).

The most common styles that most self-published authors use is:

- Manual or workbook

- Narrative Style: this is also known as a story telling style

- Humor: both written and graphical

- Specialty: these are usually reports, instruction sets, and mandated formats

- Items in an anthology (collected works)

- Interviews with experts or celebrities in a defined area of interest

- Letters from people about a specific topic compiled into a book

- Articles about a specific topic compiled into a complete book

- Technical writing

- Travel writing

- Fiction: stories and imaginary accounts of just about anything

- Non-Fiction: factual recounting of events, people, or things

Self-Publishing for the Clueless® 2nd Edition
The Workbook

Notes:

Self-Publishing for the Clueless® 2nd Edition
The Workbook

Examples of Different Types of Books

Rapid Ways to Create Information Products

Creating A Question And Answer Audio Product

Most accomplished people are constantly being asked questions and are giving away the answers for free.

Here's a method of capturing and packaging your knowledge in a hurry so you can sell it at a profit.

- Write down your area of expertise. For instance *chicken plucking*

- Write down the questions that people ask you about your area of expertise

- Write down the answers to these questions

- Locate a professional speaker that can interview you (ask you the questions)

- Arrange for a recording location and have the speaker interview you by asking the questions that you have prepared

- Have the audio recording edited, add music if applicable, have a jacket and face label created, and make copies.

Congratulations! You now have an audio product entitled:

Everything You Ever Wanted To Know About Chicken Plucking

Self-Publishing for the Clueless® 2nd Edition
The Workbook

Notes:

Self-Publishing for the Clueless® 2nd Edition
The Workbook

Book Bonus!!!

Have the audio material transcribed, edit the material, and follow the instructions below for printing the world's least expensive book have a cover created, and now you have the printed version of:

Everything You Ever Wanted To Know About Chicken Plucking

How To Publish the World's Least Expensive Printed Book

Although possibly acceptable for retail distribution, this isn't designed for that.

This is the kind of book that you'll usually find in business environments, educational venues, and religious outlooks, direct sales from a Web site and professional seminars and workshops.

Now that I've got that out of the way, let's take a look at just exactly what I'm talking about.

The picture shows a 5½" x 8½" book than can have a full color cover and plenty of content that will justify charging $5 or more for the book.

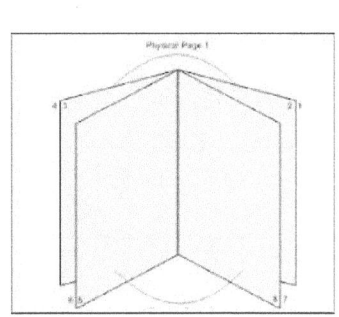

The interesting part about this particular book format, is that it's inexpensive to create (approximately 10¢ to 50¢), can have as few as eight pages, as many as 32 pages, and can be a combination of color, black and white, or just about any combination of the two that you could want.

Instructions to create a booklet using Microsoft Word:

The best way to start when you create a booklet is with a new, blank document so that you have better control over the placement of text, graphics, and other elements.

You can add a book fold to an existing document, but you may need to reposition some elements once the book fold is in place.

- Start a new, blank document.

- On the File menu, click Page Setup, and then click the Margins tab.

- In the Multiple pages list, select **book fold**.

Self-Publishing for the Clueless® 2nd Edition
The Workbook

Notes:

Self-Publishing for the Clueless® 2nd Edition
The Workbook

- If you're doing a book with mostly text, adding a border makes the finished piece look a lot snazzier.

- Add text, graphics, headers or footers (header and footer: a header, which can consist of text or graphics, appears at the top of every page in a section).

- Footers appear at the bottom of every page.

- Headers and footers often contain page numbers, chapter titles, dates, and author names and other elements to identify your document.

You're working in Word and that means all of its features including the spell checker, grammar checker, hyphenation and justification features are automatically at your disposal.

When you create your booklet content, keep in mind that the content is going to be printed differently than a normal document. Page 1 and 4 will be printed on the same side, as Page 2 and 3 will be on the opposite side.

Each page size will be shrunk to the size of half of normal page in landscape mode. The image below should help illustrate the finished product.

When you are ready to print Click File then Print and change the printing preference to the correct setting for your printer.

If your printer can automatically re-feed itself printed documents then use one of the Print On Both Sides settings, but if your printer requires you to manually re-insert your paper Select Manually Print on Both Sides.

NOTE: You can continue adding pages and design your booklet to be as large as you like, but anything over eight sheets of paper (32 pages) will start to creep out of the cover.

Here are the resources you'll need for these books:

Long-neck stapler for binding: (inventory #285535; available from www.OfficeDepot.com for $29.95).

Clip art and graphics: www.allfree-clipart.com Home to 25,000 free clip art images.

White card stock for covers: 65 lb., 8½" x 11", Stardust White, pack of 250; gives covers a crisp, professional look. (Inventory #423983; available from www.officeDepot.com for $14.95).

Self-Publishing for the Clueless® 2nd Edition
The Workbook

Notes:

Self-Publishing for the Clueless® 2nd Edition
The Workbook

High gloss photo paper for covers: 8½" x 11" coated surface, pack of 50; great for printing covers with high impact pictures, Internet images, color illustrations and digital photos. (available from www.shop4tech.com for $12.50)

Typical costs for a single copy using your own Inkjet or LaserJet printer:

Mini-Book		
8 double sided printed sheets	8 x .01	= .08
1 single or double sided sheet for the cover	1 x .01	= .01
Ink	.01	= .01
Cost for 32 page mini-book		**.10**

Add Hard Stock Cover		
8 double-sided printed sheets	8 x .01	= .08
Add a hard stock cover	1 x .06	= .06
Ink	.01	= .01
Cost for 32 page mini-book		**.15**

Add Gloss Cover		
8 double sided printed sheets	8 x .01	= .08
Add a gloss cover	1 x .24	= .24
Ink	.01	= .01
Cost for 32 page mini-book		**.33**

The Acronym Technique for Writing a Book

Many books, products, and programs become known by an acronym which often turns into a trademark. A great way to define a book about your area of expertise is to use the acronym as a chapter guideline.

This process will help you rapidly extract a list of elements that you can use as complete chapters or points of interest to be included and works because you probably know a great deal about your chosen topic but are simply having trouble deciding just exactly what you want to write about and include in your book.

Let's say that your area of expertise is *Government Procurement*. A word that is commonly used in conjunction with this process is **conformance.** By using the word, **conformance,** we can create an outline and definitions for the chapters to be filled in and expanded:

Self-Publishing for the Clueless® 2nd Edition
The Workbook

Notes:

Self-Publishing for the Clueless® 2nd Edition
The Workbook

Letter	Chapter Heading	Explanation of the Chapter's Content
C	*Continuity*	An explanation of why **CONTINUITY** of all the efforts involved result in a smoother procurement process
O	*Opportunities*	An explanation of the **OPPORTUNITIES** available to streamline the procurement process to save both money and time
N	*Negotiation*	An explanation of how to implement and utilize effective **NEGOTIATION** techniques in the procurement process
F	*Financial*	An explanation of how the **FINANCIAL** aspects of procurement are directly and indirectly affected by the processes and procedures used in procurement
O	*Order*	An explanation of how the **ORDER** processing system works and why it's essential to effective procurement
R	*Resistance*	An explanation of how properly defined and implemented procurement systems help to overcome the **RESISTANCE** to its use by all parties involved
M	*Methods*	An explanation of the different **METHODS** of procurement and when different ones should be utilized for maximum efficiency
A	*Application*	An explanation of how different **APPLICATIONS** require different procurement methodologies in order to achieve maximum effectiveness
N	*Notification*	An explanation of the different **NOTIFICATION** procedures for letting prospective bidders, bidders, and award recipients know about pertinent information, meetings, discussions, and awards.
C	*Content*	An explanation of how the **CONTENT** of a procurement document can be streamlines for greater efficiency in evaluating the compliance of bidders
E	*Efficiency*	An explanation of why greater **EFFICIENCY** will be realized when proper procedure is followed in the procurement process

You can repeat the process two or more times with different acronyms to produce more chapters or modules. Once you have several modules, you can pick and choose the ones you want to use.

Self-Publishing for the Clueless® 2nd Edition
The Workbook

Notes:

Self-Publishing for the Clueless® 2nd Edition
The Workbook
Part 9 Book Categories

All books whether distributed on paper or electronically are filed and categorized by a topic or category. In order to make sure that your materials are properly indexed and subsequently found by interested buyers, you must determine which category or categories your materials are to be listed under and add that category information to your materials.

If you are printing a paper book, this category must appear in the upper left hand corner of the back cover so the person stocking the shelves knows where to put it. If you are printing an E-book, the category information must accompany the online listing information so that it's properly categorized and indexed on the seller's Web site.

The following is a current list of **TOP LEVEL** book categories. On computerized lists like the one on CreateSpace (https://www.createspace.com/en/community/message/140475) – once you select the top level, the sub-levels will appear.

Entertainment & Leisure
- Arts and Cinema
- Astrology
- Automobiles
- Cartoon
- Cooking
- Counterculture
- Computing/Internet
- Do-It-Yourself
- Drugs
- Gambling
- Gold Mining Camps
- Party Games
- Pets
- Sexuality
- Sports
- Travel

Business & Finance
- Bankruptcy
- Business/Marketing
- Career
- Computing/Internet
- Employment
- Film Production
- Finance/Money
- Home Buyers
- Real Estate

- Strategic Planning

Hobbies
- Antiques
- Collectibles
- Cooking
- Do-It-Yourself

Law & Order
- Criminal Justice
- Law

Fiction
- General
- Adventure
- Horror
- Humor
- Literature
- Mystery
- Romance
- SciFi / Fantasy
- Suspense
- Young Adult

History
- African American
- Ancient Egypt
- Autobiography/Biography
- Counterculture
- Folk History
- History - General
- Holocaust
- Judaic
- Memoirs
- Military

- Revisionist History

Self -
- Experiences
- Growth
- Help
- Motivational
- Sexuality

Special Interest
- Gay / Lesbian
- Gun Control
- Politically Incorrect
- Politics
- Sexuality
- Transgender

Health & Living
- Abuse
- Aging
- Alcoholism
- Care Giving
- Disability
- Drugs
- Family Values
- Health/Fitness
- Health/Nutrition
- Holistic Health
- Learning Disability
- Lifestyle
- Marriage/Relationships
- Medical

- Meditation
- Mental Health
- Parenting
- Sexuality
- Women's Issues

General Interest
- Adventure
- Americana
- Chapter Books
- Children's
- Christian
- Counterculture
- Drugs
- Education
- Environment
- Essay
- Inspirational
- Nature
- New Age
- Philosophy
- Poetry
- Psychology
- Quotations
- Religion
- Reluctant Readers
- Revelation
- Sexuality
- Sociology
- Spiritual
- Uncategorized

Self-Publishing for the Clueless® 2nd Edition
The Workbook

Notes:

Self-Publishing for the Clueless® 2nd Edition
The Workbook
Part 10 References and Resources

These resources represent people and organizations that we've used successfully for many years.

We recommend their services and products because they're reasonably priced, high quality, and will work with you rather than for you—an important element for the self-publisher.

1. Free and Fee Website services www.Weebly.com

2. Printing services of all types and quantities: Copyland; Andre Rosemburg www.onedaycopy.com 310-479-3957

3. Print-On Demand services – CreateSpace® www.createspace.com

4. Book Cover and Graphic Design Services Leslie Sears www.LesIsMore.us 310-245-6411

5. Royalty free clip art www.Clipart.com

6. Typing and Transcription Services Nancy Gillespie nancyJG5@cox.net 760-945-6667

7. Blank CDS, DVDS, and other Multi-media related products www.shop4tech.com

8. CD and DVD Duplication and packaging Services http://cheapcdduplications.com/ info@cheapcdduplications.com 800-836-796

9. ISBN numbers www.bowker.com

10. Copyright registration www.LOC.gov

11. Trademark registration www.USPTO.gov

Self-Publishing for the Clueless® 2nd Edition
The Workbook

Notes:

Self-Publishing for the Clueless® 2nd Edition
The Workbook

The Full version of the manual, downloadable at http://tinyurl.com/lgze57h (**Password CPM7MFR**) contains the complete 267 page manual Self-Publishing for the Clueless® 2nd Edition (Table of Contents shown below)

Contents

Part 1 – General information	9
Why Be Published?	9
Types Of Published Materials	10
What's The Difference Between Royalty Publishing And Self-Publishing?	11
Why Self-Publish Your Materials?	12
The Advantages Of Self-Publishing	13
The Disadvantages Of Self-Publishing	13
Publishing Industry Statistics	15
Part 2 - What Publishing Is All About	19
Basic Information About Publishing	19
The First Decisions	21
Part 3 - Publishing Details	23
The Cover	23
The Title And Category	24
The Category Title	25
Sizes Of Books	25
Font Style And Size	26
The Best Fonts For An Effective Presentation	28
Margins	30
Illustrations, Pictures And Graphics	31
Headlines And Bullet Points	32
Copyrighted Images: Don't Use Without Permission	33
Practical Considerations For Adding Graphics To Your Published Works	34
Color, Halftone Grey And Black And White Art	36
Indexing Your Book	37
Paper Stock	37
Cover Stock	40
Boilerplate Items	41
ISBN	43
Barcodes	44
Part 4 - Types Of Books, Binding, And Printing Processes	47
Binding Styles (Aka The Cover)	47
Printing Types	49
Part 5 - How To Price Your Products	53
SRP (Suggested Retail Price)	53
Setting The Retail Price For Your Book	54
Factors That Influence Pricing	59
Part 6 - E-Books	65
What Is E-Publishing?	65
The Advantages To E-Publishing	66
Welcome To The World Of Tablet Computing	67

Self-Publishing for the Clueless® 2nd Edition
The Workbook

Notes:

Self-Publishing for the Clueless® 2nd Edition
The Workbook

Popular E-Publishing Formats	77
E-Book Readers	77
E-Book Formats	86
Free Software To Create EPUB Digital Books	88
EPUB Versus PDF - The Pros And Cons For E-Publishing	92
Multi-Media E-books	94
How Do You Create An E-Book?	96
6 Expert Tips On Designing A Great Book Cover	99
Part 7 - Audio Products And Podcasting	105
Background Of The Medium	105
Where Do You Get Audio Recordings?	108
Software For Recording And Editing Audio	109
Hardware For Recording And Editing Audio	110
Delivery Mediums For Audio Products	111
Part 8 - Video Products And Podcasting	115
Why Use Video?	115
The 8 Fundamental Uses For Video In Business	117
Video Podcasting	120
Digital Video Cameras	130
Video Editing Software	131
Part 9 - Distributing And Marketing Your Products	135
The Hierarchy Of Bookstores	136
How To Sell Your E-book In The Apple I-book Store	137
Ways Of Selling Your Work	142
Promoting Your Book On Talk Radio	143
Promoting Your E-Publications Through BLOGs	148
Free Support And Promotional Downloads	149
Selling Your Published Materials	149
Listing With Major Distribution Chains	150
Publishing For Kindle	152
Barnes And Noble	153
Baker & Taylor	153
Part 10 - Welcome To The World Of E-Commerce	155
Web Sites, PayPal, And Pay-Per-Download	155
How To Create A Free Web Site	155
The Shopping Cart	157
Pay-Per-Download Service	158
QR Codes - The Easiest Way To Link People To Your Web Site!	159
Part 11 - The Legal Stuff	163
Trademarks	163
Filing A Trademark	164
Trademarks And The Internet	167
Copyrights	170
Securing A Copyright	171
How Long Do Copyrights Last?	172
What Rights Are Cover Or Protected?	173
Not Protected By Copyright	175
Derivative Work	176

Self-Publishing for the Clueless® 2nd Edition
The Workbook

Notes:

Self-Publishing for the Clueless® 2nd Edition
The Workbook

Copyright Notice Elements	177
Fair Use	178
Work-Made-For-Hire	178
DRM	180
Resources For DRM	181
The Law As Viewed From The Author's Standpoint	183
How To Get Permission To Quote Someone In Your Book	185
Plagiarism And How To Avoid It	186
What Are The Repercussions Of Committing Plagiarism?	196
Permission To Quote	197
Part 12 - Types And Styles Of Books	199
Part 13 – Rapid Ways To Create Information Products	203
A Tips Booklet	203
Creating A Question And Answer Audio Product	204
How To Publish The World's Least Expensive Printed Book	205
The Acronym Technique For Writing A Book	208
Part 14 - References And Resources	209
Part 15 – Appendices	211
Appendix 01 Print-On-Demand Companies	211
Appendix 02 - Book Categories	212
Appendix 03 - Places To Obtain Graphics For Your Products	218
Appendix 04 - Selected Podcast Hosting. Some Offer Free Podcast Hosting	222
Appendix 05 - Additional Places To Offer Your Materials For Sale	223
Appendix 06 - 10 Ways To Promote Your Podcast Free	237
Appendix 07 - Example Of A "Boilerplate" Page	242
Appendix 08 - Selling Books To Airport Shops	245
Appendix 09 - Do You Want To Start Your Own Publishing Company?	252
Appendix 10- The Pros And Cons Of Pseudonyms	254
Appendix 11- How To File A Fictitious Business Name Statement	261
Appendix 12 - Library Of Congress Registration	263
Appendix 13 - The Golden Rules For Amazon.com Formatting	264

Self-Publishing for the Clueless® 2nd Edition
The Workbook

Notes:

Self-Publishing for the Clueless® 2nd Edition
The Workbook

Visit our Web site at www.RoundsMiller.com and check out the section entitled:
Articles of Interest

As new and exciting changes occur in the Self-Publishing and E-Publishing arenas, we post articles of interest to keep you up to date.

Contact Information:

Mike Rounds and Nancy Miller
Rounds, Miller and Associates
6318 Ridgepath Court; Rancho Palos Verdes, CA 90275-3248
310-544-9502
www.RoundsMiller.com
Mike@RoundsMiller.com

Self-Publishing for the Clueless® 2nd Edition
The Workbook

Notes:

Self-Publishing for the Clueless® 2nd Edition
The Workbook
Book Shepherding Services

A Book Shepherd is someone who can take your manuscript through all the processes to a finished book.

Although you can always do it all yourself it's a proven fact that having a guide that's **"been there and done that"** to **"Shepard"** you through the different processes help insure that you actually get you published material to market in the shortest amount of time.

The objective is to ensure that during the project the coordination and supervision of all the tasks be monitored and that everybody involved be kept informed of the progress, problems, and successes.

The program consists of regular meetings, teleconferencing, and e-mail coaching as needed, and includes tasks and assignments that you will need to complete in order to assure your complete success. We'll throw in an UNLIMITED number of 10 minute consultations and as much e-mail assistance as you can write for the duration of the program.

Our responsibility will be to take your basic book files plus any graphics that you want inserted, perform basic editing, grammar and spell checking, and format the book for both paper publishing and electronic publishing as shown below.

You're actually going to have the same material formatted into four different formats for your specified needs:

A fully edited Word® file that will be used for all editing, layout, formatting, and corrections.

1. A PDF format book based on the edited word® file; fully compatible with, and ready for, paper printing. The final size is proposed to be either 5.5" x 8" or 8.5" x 11" with a perfect bound cover; black and white interior, full color gloss cover, and an estimated page count of approximately 400 pages.
2. A PDF format book based on the edited Word® file; fully compatible with, and ready for, pay-per-download from your site and most other Pay-per-download sites; full color interior, full color cover.
3. Your book and cover, formatted and submitted to Amazon's *CreateSpace*™ for their Print-on-Demand services including posting an instant order button on your website.

In addition to our services, you'll be looking at the following estimated charges:

ISBN Numbers - $125 – This is obtained directly, by you, from Bowker.com.
  Note: We can obtain a free listing if you agree to only print through CreateSpace

Self-Publishing for the Clueless® 2nd Edition
The Workbook

Web site hosting and domain charges – These will be approximately $5.00 per month plus $3 per month for a custom domain name and will require that you sign up for the service using your credit card.

- We will work with you to select, and register, a suitable domain name for the site. If you have problems with this, we will walk you through the process via phone.
- **Pay-Per-Download e-book delivery services** - These will be approximately $5.00 per month and will require that you sign up for the service using your credit card. If you have problems with this, we will walk you through the process via phone.
- **Credit card/merchant account services** – These are available from Paypal.com. These services are free but require that you sign up for the service using your credit card.
- **Cover design charges** (if needed) – $300-$500
- **Printing charges** – Estimated to be approximately $5.00-$6.00 (or less) per book in a 100 piece quantity.

We'll create a basic web site for you to modify and perform the posting of the web site for you and the book to include the insertion of following elements which you will be free to modify at your discretion:

- The author
- The book
- Excerpts from the book
- Order page with pay-per-download capability
- A Blog for comments and feedback
- Contact information

Once it's complete, we'll supply you with a list of on-line, e-book resellers where you can actually post the book for resale as well as supplying you with the PDF files for hard copy reproduction.

As a general rule, from the time we receive the final copy until you have books available will be six weeks or less assuming, of course, that as we send material to you for final revisions that you make whatever corrections are necessary and return it to us with 4-5 days.

The fees for our basic book shepherding services as described herein are $2,100 and our terms are full payment for services ($2,100) required to begin the work as described herein.

OPTION:

As an option, we can format your book for Amazon's Kindle as well. This will include:

Amazon *Kindle®,* for their proprietary electronic download format; black and white interior and cover.

Self-Publishing for the Clueless® 2nd Edition
The Workbook

What we're going to do is break down and strip out all of the original formatting and reformat the book, complete with the graphics placement, for the different delivery venues as specified.

Once it's complete, **_we'll actually post the books on the site for you_** as a part of the project plus we'll send the PDF files for hard copy reproduction.

The fees for our optional items as described above are $300.

Self-Publishing for the Clueless® 2nd Edition
The Workbook

Publishers Haven

Introducing **Publisher's Haven**™ – The web site with the answers you need to get your books and other materials finished and sold.

www.PublishersHaven.com

We're Podcasting! –On November 20th, 2014, **we began podcasting** twice a week to provide you with the latest information about latest changes in the world of publishing and to help you market your materials

Paste our RSS feed into your own player or play directly from our site at
http://www.publishershaven.com/our-podcast.html

RSS Feed: http://MikeRounds.podbean.com/feed

Tons of FREE stuff!

At **Publishers Haven**™ we post all kinds of *Free Stuff* each month to help you with your publishing efforts including articles and resources about:

- How to create your own author/publisher web site for FREE!
- The three types of editing: Which one does your manuscript need?
- Photo and video Release
- How to get permission to quote someone in your book
- Free translation software
- Instructions for publishing your e-book on Kindle
- How to sell your eBook in the Apple iBook store
- 85 places to offer your books and eBooks
- And lots more

6318 Ridgepath Court
Rancho Palos Verdes, CA 90275-3248
310.544.9502
www.RoundsMiller.com

Business, Technology and Organizing Training Specialists

PRODUCT CATALOG

Audio/Video Toolkit

Complete Windows® software series including: **Banner Maker** PDF with video instruction for making your own web site banner using Microsoft Publisher®; links and information for 100,000+ royalty free graphics, sources for free music for videos and slideshows. **CamStudio**™ Video Screen recording software. **VideoSoft**™ Complete audio/video editing and conversion suite including 55 separate conversion programs for video, audio, and mobile devices. **Audacity**™ Audio recording and editing software.

Audio/Data CD+   **$24.95**

Book Marketing for the Clueless®

Want to sell your books, CDs and DVDs for a profit? This audio/PDF CD includes databases of over 500 catalogs and outlets that market books and instructions on how to solicit your publications including how to be listed with Amazon.com for free.

Audio/Data CD+   ISBN 978-1-891440-49-6   **$24.95**
eBook*   ISBN 978-1-891440-94-6   **$9.95**

Business Training for the Clueless®

A complete course about becoming a six figure a year business trainer. Contains a complete PDF manual, workbook, training aids, exercise, games, on-screen timing software, and royalty free audio clips.

Book & Data CD+   ISBN 978-1-891440-85-4   **$69.95**
eBook*   ISBN 978-1-891440-96-0   **$9.95**

Cash From Your Clutter

A manual filled with resources to help you turn your excess stuff into cash. Includes information on what sells, where to sell your excess stuff, how to place a realistic sales value on your stuff, the best time to sell your stuff, how to donate for tax deductions, a special section on how to sell your timeshare property and much more.

eBook*   ISBN 978-1-891440-79-3   **$9.95**

The Clutter Bug Attacks Christmas Clutter™

If there's one time of the year our homes and lives become more cluttered, it's Christmas. Here are quick and easy ways to simplify Christmas, including how to: plan and organize your Christmas, get your card and gift lists under control, simplify your gift giving, handle the gifts you receive, and get rid of Christmas clutter!

Book   ISBN 978-1-891440-74-8   **$15.95**
eBook*   ISBN 978-1-891440-84-7   **$9.95**

The Clutter Bug Attacks Junk Mail, Spam and Telemarketers™

Overwhelmed by Junk Mail? Spam? Telemarketers? These can all be stopped! Current, verified information with visual examples for quick and easy understanding. The first book ever to show you how to get off of political mailings, plus proven and structured processes for both eliminating and retaining communications.

eBook*   ISBN 978-1-891440-81-6   **$9.95**

*eBooks contain a complete book in PDF for use on all Mac & Windows PCs, including desktops, notebooks/laptops, netbooks & tablets.
+All data files are in PDF format, playable/viewable on Windows and Mac, audio files are in Wave format playable on standard CD players.

The Clutter Bug Investigates Coupons, Discounts, and Deals™

A complete manual describing the coupon process and how to use them to save 35 to 85 percent on your shopping. Includes complete detailed illustrations and examples on where to find coupons, types of coupons, store policies for coupons, deals and discounts, rebates and refunds, and rewards and loyalty cards.

Book	ISBN 978-1-891440-77-9	$24.95
eBook*	ISBN 978-1-891440-82-3	$9.95

Clutterology® Getting Rid of Clutter and Getting Organized! 4th Edition

Revised and Expanded! A complete manual on how to get organized, set up and maintain manageable filing systems, and eliminate clutter that gets in your way. Provides some of the simplest, easiest and most practical advice on how to remove the clutter from your life and get organized.

Book	ISBN 978-1-891440-89-2	$34.95
eBook*	ISBN 978-1-891440-71-7	$9.95

Highlights of Clutterology®

This audio CD has over 60 minutes of tips, tricks, insights, and stories about getting rid of your clutter and getting organized. It's ideal for reinforcement to remind you that getting organized is a step-by-step process that you can accomplish if you take it easy and stick with it.

Audio CD+	ISBN 978-1-891440-44-1	$19.95

How to Become a Clutterologist™

Do label makers and shelf dividers make you smile? Use your aptitude for organization to change lives and turn your decluttering skills into a moneymaking career; become a professional organizer! Includes the tools and knowledge you need to succeed in the professional organizer industry: organizing specialties, understanding the Clutter-Hoarding Scale, how to structure your business for SUCCESS, business licensing and insurance.

Book	ISBN 978-1-891440-56-4	$34.95
eBook*	ISBN 978-1-891440-68-7	$9.95

Consulting for the Clueless®

In today's business climate, consultants are flourishing while others can't find a job. This book will show you how to profitably leverage your experience into a six-figure income with minimal investment. Includes DVD with consulting seminar, PDF copy of Marketing the One-Person Business, and support software.

Book and Windows Software DVD	$39.95

Contracts and Agreements for Inventors

Over a dozen of the most utilized agreements to help ensure that what's yours stays yours. With the help of an attorney, they contain everything you'll need from a confidentiality agreement to work-for-hire agreements, assignment of rights, and partnership agreements. Comes with instructions for usage, filling out, and filing where applicable.

Data CD+	$19.95

E-Commerce for the Clueless®

Complete manual plus instruction program on CD that includes Flash® video on what e-commerce is and isn't, what's required to get involved, how to set up a web site page for e-commerce, setting up a FREE PayPal account and product purchase buttons, and how to set up a pay-per-download account to sell e-books and other information products directly from your web site. Includes royalty free background music clips

Book	ISBN 978-1-891440-80-9	$39.95
Data CD+	ISBN 978-1-891440-78-6	$24.95

---

*eBooks contain a complete book in PDF for use on all Mac & Windows PCs, including desktops, notebooks/laptops, netbooks & tablets.
+All data files are in PDF format, playable/viewable on Windows and Mac, audio files are in Wave format playable on standard CD players.

Fishin' With A Net, 8th Edition
Learn the elements of designing a Web site that actually works for you and can be created in less than four hours. Covers what the Web really is, what to put on your site to be successful, and how to link with the search engines quickly and easily.

Book   ISBN 978-1-891440-97-7   **$24.95**

Headline Creator™ Pro Suite
"Your headline can result in 80 percent or more of the effectiveness of your ad or sales page!" Automatically generates time-tested, proven, results-oriented headlines based on the greatest headlines in history. . . and does it in 17 seconds!

Windows Software CD$^+$ **$39.95**

How To Sell Your Inventions for Cash, 3rd Edition
Everything you need to know to be a successful inventor! Takes your idea from inception through the licensing process to a manufacturer for royalties. Learn how to protect your inventions using patents, trademarks, copyrights, and other legal instruments, determine if you're ready to offer your idea, and how to find and solicit manufacturers who are interested in your ideas.

Book   ISBN 978-1-891440-59-5   **$24.95**
eBook*   ISBN 978-1-891440-63-2   **$9.95**
Audio CD$^+$ ISBN 978-1-891440-28-1   **$39.95**

Intellectual Property Protection for the Clueless®
CD contains 3 hours of audio plus 100s of pages in PDF format on trademarks, patents and copyright. Includes forms for filing without an attorney! *Bonus: How to Apply for an Innovation Research Grant!* This audio is in MP3 format playable with the Windows Media Player or comparable MP3 software.

MP3 Audio/Data CD$^+$ ISBN 978-1-891440-67-0   **$59.95**

Marketing the One-Person Business, 2nd Edition
A one-person business is different from any other because you have to do the business PLUS get the business. Contains complete information about setup, operation, independent contractor criteria and forms, fee setting, consulting, public speaking, seminars, contracts and agreements.

Book   ISBN 978-1-891440-29-8   **$24.95**
eBook*   ISBN 978-1-891440-88-5   **$9.95**

Mechanics of Starting a Home-Based Business, 2nd Edition
A home-based business is a business whose primary office is in the owner's home. Explains the realities of starting and operating a home business and including resources for taxes, licenses, and advertising plus computer operated business you can start and run.

Book   ISBN 978-1-891440-64-9   **$34.95**
eBook*   ISBN 978-1-891440-70-0   **$9.95**

Photo Manipulator Software
Shrink Pic™ software automatically reduces the size of photos for email, blogging and web galleries. No set up, no operating instructions, just send your photos normally and Shrink Pic™ does the work. Paint Shop Pro™ 4 is an easy to use photo editing program that let's you enhance your photos and create professional-looking images.

Windows Software CD$^+$ **$19.95**

Professional Speaking for the Clueless®
Do you want to be paid to speak? This book explains the REAL business of professional speaking and how to make six figures a year without huge marketing and advertising costs. Includes dozens of resources, databases, and complete explanations of how to locate speaking opportunities and market to them.

Audio/Data CD$^+$ ISBN 978-1-891440-53-3   **$24.95**
eBook*   ISBN 978-1-891440-91-5   **$9.95**

**eBooks contain a complete book in PDF for use on all Mac & Windows PCs, including desktops, notebooks/laptops, netbooks & tablets.*
$^+$*All data files are in PDF format, playable/viewable on Windows and Mac, audio files are in Wave format playable on standard CD players.*

Profitable Publishing for the Clueless®

The complete 3 CD set containing everything you need to know to generate, protect, and market your printed work. See full description for each item.

Disk 1 - Self-Publishing for the Clueless®
Disk 2 - Trademarks & Copyrights for the Clueless®
Disk 3 - Book Marketing for the Clueless®

Audio/Data CD+   ISBN 978-1-891440-51-9   **$59.95**

Project Management for the Clueless®

Zipped file containing a 1-hour audio seminar and all of the documents you'll need to organize, plan and budget most projects in three hours or less.

eBook*   ISBN 978-1-891440-95-3   **$9.95**

Self-Publishing for the Clueless®, 2nd Edition

Complete workbook on self-publishing, e-publishing, and a secured access to a 270 page manual with the latest information, resources, and insider tips about the world of e-publishing including how to be e-published in a week.

Workbook and Data CD+   ISBN 978-1-891440-99-1   **$34.95**

Trademarks & Copyrights for the Clueless®

Trademarks are the mark of your trade and copyrights address the laws allowing you the rights to make copies of your work. Contains printable forms and examples, explaining how to protect your works plus what material of others you can use without fear of legal problems.

Audio/Data CD+   ISBN 978-1-891440-30-4   **$24.95**
eBook*   ISBN 978-1-891440-92-2   **$9.95**

Venture Capital for the Clueless®

Venture Capital is available for all types of businesses and your ability to tap into it depends on your ability to write a business plan that sells you and your ideas to the people with the money. Includes explanations, samples, printable forms, and sources of venture funding.

Audio/Data CD+   ISBN 978-1-891440-31-1   **$24.95**
eBook*   ISBN 978-1-891440-93-9   **$9.95**

Virtual Business for the Clueless®

Use the Latest Technology to Improve Business, Sales, and Communications. Computers have given us virtual tools that you can use to improve your productivity, whether you are a volunteer organization, a small business or a large enterprise. Covers: PowerPoint Programs - Beyond the Basics; Audio and Video Podcasts, Tele-Seminars and Webinars; Green Screen and On-Demand Programming; and more!

Book   ISBN 978-1-891440-63-2   **$39.95**

Whadda We Do NOW?™

Provides quick fixes for failing businesses. Learn how to quickly and easily figure out what's wrong so you can stop guessing and start implementing solutions. The information is practical, easy to understand, and readily implementable if you're serious about getting your business into a positive cash flow position-NOW!

Book   ISBN 978-1-891440-66-3   **$29.95**

---

*eBooks contain a complete book in PDF for use on all Mac & Windows PCs, including desktops, notebooks/laptops, netbooks & tablets.
+All data files are in PDF format, playable/viewable on Windows and Mac, audio files are in Wave format playable on standard CD players.

Training Kits

Become a Professional Organizer

If you'd like to get into the lucrative world of professional organizing, then everything you'll need to setup a business, get clients, and operate profitably is on the list below. Contains:

Books: How to Become a Clutterologist™, Clutterology® Getting Rid of Clutter and Getting Organized!; Fishin' with a Net™, How to Develop an Effective Web Site; Mechanics of Starting a Home-Based Business™, and Self-Publishing for the Clueless® 2nd edition

Plus DVD/CDs: Headline Creator™ Pro Suite, Marketing the One-Person Business™, and Highlights of Clutterology©

Kit $261.95

Entrepreneurship

Do you dream of working for yourself? This kit includes everything for setting up a home-based business, getting organized, raising venture capital to fund the efforts, scheduling and managing your time, and ways to market your skills profitably.

Contains: Books: Mechanics of Starting a Home-Based Business™, Clutterology® Getting Rid of Clutter and Getting Organized!, Fishin' with a Net™, How to Develop an Effective Web Site, and Self-Publishing for the Clueless® 2nd edition.

Plus DVD/CDs: Marketing the One-Person Business™, Headline Creator™ Pro Suite, Professional Speaking for the Clueless®, and Venture Capital for the Clueless®.

Kit $169.95

Invention Marketing

The material listed is endorsed by the SBA as "The only legitimate program for marketing inventions that we've ever seen." It explains how to organize and manage your invention process, protect them with patents, trademarks and copyrights, set up a home business, offer your ideas for sale, plus information for raising venture capital to fund your projects.

Contains: Books: How to Sell Your Inventions for Cash™ and Mechanics of Starting a Home-Based Business.

Plus DVD/CDs: How to Sell Your Inventions for Cash, Contracts and Agreements for Inventors, Venture Capital for the Clueless®, and Trademarks & Copyrights for the Clueless®.

Kit $161.95

Professional Speaking

If you're interested in professional speaking, you'll find everything needed to get profitable bookings including places to get booked and instructions on how to do it! Includes over 1,700 pages of printable information, eight hours of video, four hours of audio, and hundreds of support resources.

Contains: Books: Mining the College Market, Mechanics of Starting A Home-Based Business, and Fishin' with a Net™, How to Develop an Effective Web Site, Self-Publishing for the Clueless® 2nd edition, and Business Training for the Clueless® (plus CDs),

Plus DVD/CDs: Headline Creator™ Pro Suite, Marketing the One-Person Business, Professional Speaking for the Clueless®.

Kit $461.95

Raising Venture Capital

Looking for money or backing for a new idea or enterprise? Confused about what to do and how to approach investors? We've assembled the materials needed to establish proprietary rights to your innovations; plan, budget, organize and schedule your project; prepare a business plan and shop it to people with investment capital. Contains:

Books: Clutterology® Getting Rid of Clutter and Getting Organized! and Mechanics of Starting a Home-Based Business, Fishin' with a Net™, How to Develop an Effective Web Site, and Self-Publishing for the Clueless® 2nd Edition.

Plus DVD/CDs: Trademarks & Copyrights for the Clueless®, Venture Capital for the Clueless®, Headline Creator™ Pro Suite, and Highlights of Clutterology©.

Kit $191.95

---

*eBooks contain a complete book in PDF for use on all Mac & Windows PCs, including desktops, notebooks/laptops, netbooks & tablets.
+All data files are in PDF format, playable/viewable on Windows and Mac, audio files are in Wave format playable on standard CD players.

Self-Publishing

You CAN have a book ready to sell in 30 days with these practical products... guaranteed! Contains everything needed including pre-configured scheduling and budgeting charts to get your own project finished in record time with a minimal amount of expense and hassles.

Contains: Books: Mechanics of Starting A Home-Based Business, Fishin' with a Net™, How to Develop an Effective Web Site, and Self-Publishing for the Clueless® 2nd edition.

Plus DVD/CDs: Trademarks & Copyrights for the Clueless®, Book Marketing for the Clueless®, and Headline Creator™ Pro Suite.

Kit $261.95

Web Site Development Software Suite

No software you use to create your Web site will contain everything you need, so we've assembled the "stuff they left out." This suite of software and resources will help make your Web site work efficiently and get the response it deserves. These products have a proven track record in the world of Web design, marketing and advertising.

Contains: DVD/CDs: AV Toolkit; Photo Manipulator Toolkit, Headline Creator™ Pro Suite, Trademarks & Copyrights for the Clueless®, and E-Commerce for the Clueless®.

Kit $100.00

---

*eBooks contain a complete book in PDF for use on all Mac & Windows PCs, including desktops, notebooks/laptops, netbooks & tablets.
+All data files are in PDF format, playable/viewable on Windows and Mac, audio files are in Wave format playable on standard CD players.

6318 Ridgepath Court
Rancho Palos Verdes, CA 90275-3248
310.544.9502
www.RoundsMiller.com

Business, Technology and Organizing Training Specialists

ORDER FORM

ITEM (See Catalog for Full Description)	Format	Qty.	Price
Audio/Video Toolkit	Audio/Data CD $24.95		
Book Marketing for the Clueless®	Audio/Data CD $24.95		
	eBook - Online $9.95	PURCHASE ONLINE	
Business Training for the Clueless®	Book & Data CD $69.95		
	eBook - Online $9.95	PURCHASE ONLINE	
Cash From Your Clutter	eBook - Online $9.95	PURCHASE ONLINE	
The Clutter Bug Attacks Christmas Clutter™	Book $15.95		
	eBook - Online $9.95	PURCHASE ONLINE	
The Clutter Bug Attacks Junk Mail, Spam and Telemarketers™	eBook - Online $9.95	PURCHASE ONLINE	
The Clutter Bug Investigates Coupons, Discounts, and Deals™	Book $24.95		
	eBook - Online $9.95	PURCHASE ONLINE	
Clutterology® Getting Rid of Clutter and Getting Organized!	Book $34.95		
	eBook - Online $9.95	PURCHASE ONLINE	
Highlights of Clutterology®	Audio CD $19.95		
How to Become a Clutterologist™	Book $34.95		
	eBook - Online $9.95	PURCHASE ONLINE	
Consulting for the Clueless®	Book/Software DVD $39.95		
Contracts and Agreements for Inventors	Data CD $19.95		
E-Commerce for the Clueless®	Data CD $24.95		
	Book $24.95		
Fishin' With A Net	Book $24.95		
Headline Creator™ Pro Suite	Software CD $39.95		
How To Sell Your Inventions for Cash	Book $24.95		
	eBook - Online $9.95	PURCHASE ONLINE	
	Audio CD $39.95		
Intellectual Property Protection for the Clueless®	MP3 Audio/Data CD $59.95		
Marketing the One-Person Business	Book $24.95		
	eBook - Online $9.95	PURCHASE ONLINE	
Mechanics of Starting a Home-Based Business	Book $34.95		
	eBook - Online $9.95	PURCHASE ONLINE	
Photo Manipulator Software	Software CD $19.95		
Professional Speaking for the Clueless®	Audio/Data CD $24.95		
	eBook - Online $9.95	PURCHASE ONLINE	
Profitable Publishing for the Clueless®	3 Audio/Data CDs $59.95		
Project Management for the Clueless®	eBook - Online $9.95	PURCHASE ONLINE	
Self-Publishing for the Clueless®	Workbook & Data CD $34.95		

	Page 1 Sub-Total	

Trademarks & Copyrights for the Clueless®	Audio/Data CD $24.95		
	eBook - Online $9.95	PURCHASE ONLINE	
Venture Capital for the Clueless®	Audio/Data CD $24.95		
	eBook - Online $9.95	PURCHASE ONLINE	
Virtual Business for the Clueless®	Book $39.95		
Whadda We Do NOW?™	Book $29.95		
TRAINING KITS			
Become a Professional Organizer	Kit $261.95		
Entrepreneurship	Kit $169.95		
Invention Marketing	Kit $161.95		
Professional Speaking	Kit $461.95		
Raising Venture Capital	Kit $191.95		
Self-Publishing	Kit $261.95		
Web Site Development Software Suite	Kit $100.00		

E-Books are available for purchase and instant download online at www.RMACart.com/E-Books.htm

Amount from Page 1	
Sub-Total	
in CA add Sales Tax 9.75%	
Shipping	$2.95
Total	

Thank You!

Name (please print) _____

Mailing Address: _____

City, State, ZIP: _____

Tel: _____ e-Mail: _____

I authorize Rounds, Miller and Associates to charge my credit card for the items listed above

Credit Card Number: _____ exp. _____ CSS _____

Signature: _____ Date: _____

To Order By Mail:

Send completed order form and check payable to Rounds, Miller and Associates to

6318 Ridgepath Court

Rancho Palos Verdes, CA 90275

View our entire product line at www.RoundsMiller.com

www.ingramcontent.com/pod-product-compliance
Lightning Source LLC
Chambersburg PA
CBHW080739230426
43665CB00020B/2798